Walking with Shadows

(The Morphine Collection)

by John J. Whitmarsh

ISBN 1-905168-07-1

Published by Paula Brown Trading as The People's Poet
Illustrations by Karin Sköld

Printed in Great Britain by
JEMDigital Print Ltd., Kent, England

If only you could hear some of the nonsense I come out with when the liquid morphine really kicks in!... if only we kept a tape recorder going all night!!

An invitation from the author

Only you are invited to peek behind the blackout curtain of my private room, to glimpse my secret world in these, my gaudy final days where one long sunset dims then brightens the closing night time sky.
Do not fret or panic, for if I have survived so long on the inside of this bubbling cauldron, if I undergo this turmoil and befriend this chameleon mood without flinching, why then, my friend, should you fear suffering when all you need do to satisfy my request is view the ever shifting hullabaloo from the safety of without?

Contents

Bant's Carn

Where the day's last light
Pricks the distant water,
There I will lie down
To face my ever after.

As the sun sets silver
On Atlantic calm
Put me where I long to be -
Hid, and safe from harm.

Put me down to rest
Where tranquillity we knew,
And say a soft goodbye
To the man who still loves you.

John J Whitmarsh

NB: As he had requested, John Whitmarsh's ashes were scattered near Bant's Carn during a family holiday at the end of August, 2004. It was reported that the sea appeared to have writing in the waves that evening, and a lone piper piped some music as the ashes dropped into the heather.

Foreword by Paula Brown

When John Whitmarsh (People's Poet award for 2002 and author of the major poetry anthology Magic Light) began sending me poetry, written while under the influence of Morphine, I realised quite quickly that these works could become an invaluable collection.

John is, essentially, an ordinary man from Sheffield in the UK. Married to Susan for more years than either of them care to remember; John is a Father, Husband, Poet, Author of prose, Novelist, and he is living with cancer.

Because John has found a unique way of making use of the way he experiences his sudden change of life and his relationship with Morphine, it could inspire other people with cancer in ther lives or those using Morphine for other reasons to view the experiences in a more constructive way. I would also hope that the vibrant use of words and wit shown by John will diffuse some humour among some challenging observations.

This collection features prose, poetry, musings and thoughts all connected with the experience of living with cancer and the use of Morphine. Some of the works may, at first, seem difficult to read as they are extraordinarily emotional but John doesn't allow us to wallow for long - his irresistable optimism and his wicked humour are ever present.

We recognise how invaluable Morphine's contribution is to pain relief. We are merely illustrating one man's experience in verse and prose.

I would like to thank John publicly for his considerate wish to share his most private work and thoughts with us all.

NB: I have retained John's choice of font throughout, wherever possible. PB

The Colour of the Future

On looking back, I see every minute of my life crammed full and crowded to the gunnels with activity. Some blink-swift seconds contain the wealth of crushed pearl or polished ruby, while others, empty to the unobservant eye, are filled with the air of contemplation or dreams in the weaving. Some pockets of time, long or short according to the mood of the memory, may bring the redness of shame to the surface, or the remembrance of fear, or a feeling of foolishness that is hard to bear; others will glow eternal – the certificate gained, the race run, the heart stolen, the triumph of a victory snatched when success seemed impossible with odds stacked so high against. No second wasted, no moment trivial, no passing tick unmarked by a thought or a deed. These are the twin definitions of life: - the filling of time with activity; or the pouring of activity into the time allowed. Time is the mould into which the plaster of life is tipped. The shape of one becomes the shape of the other – mould and plaster are indistinguishable, inseparable.

Suddenly or predictably, but most frequently unwelcome, comes the moment when the plaster vanishes as life is snuffed out. Time's mould sits empty or, with the dead envying the living, fills up with activities and thoughts belonging to others. New races are run that I cannot compete in; new loves are experienced that I feel no heat from, new goals attained and old ones revisited through eyes that are not mine. Impotent, I will sit in the Afterlife audience with no hope of influencing outcomes. I rage, I protest, but I am powerless. Time will tick without me, and the world will live on in my absence, exactly as it lives on after the flicking out of generations stretching back to antiquity; and it will go on when the children of my children's children look back at their days and wonder whose plaster will fill their private Time's eternal mould. Envy, right or not, is the colour of my future.

John. 14th July 2003

Room

The room has no beginning;
It has no ending,
It has no bounds,
No height
Or depth
Or breadth;
It is a space without colour
Or definition;
It is a place where a step taken
Can be measured in miles
Or not measured at all,
For distances covered by a single step
Or a by a thousand
Are unpredictable
And meaningless.
Sounds cannot echo
For echoes require walls,
But this place possesses none,
None at all,
Nor any feature expected of
A conventional room
Occupying finite space.
But this is forgivable,
For my room exists not
In the inhibited cosmos
But in the miasma
Of my roving head.

The Melding of Sleep and Wakefulness

As a result of my frequent ingestion of Oramorph, a commonly prescribed brand of liquid morphine, I often find myself in a world familiar to hypnotherapists, brainwashers and – I would suppose - the keepers of lunatic asylums. This world exists simultaneously in two places at once, both of which landscapes are well known to us all. In wakefulness we experience what we like to call 'the real world'. Sights seen and words spoken here are taken as factual; rocks are solid, birds fly while sheep do not; clouds are reservoirs of water that are never capable of giving birth to angels or devils. On the other hand, the world of sleep suffers few if any constraints. Sheep not only fly, but they talk, threaten, tell jokes and quaff ale when the mood takes them! As for clouds – well, they have been known (by me) to be the breeding ground of all manner of terrifying beasties. Rocks float, seas open, silent shapes and shadows that can be seen only in peripheral vision emerge from walls to intimidate me at three in the morning or two in the afternoon, and very ordinary voices speak to me when the room is empty. If the room happens to be occupied by REAL people, the voices are not audible to any but me.

We are all used to ordinary dreams where odd things happen, and we learn to come to terms with them in our early years. The moment our eyes open, we shrug off a dream as being a sometimes pleasant, sometime frightening fantasy that has no meaning in the diurnal world. Oh that I could do that now! I awake, and the walls continue sprouting shapes; I open my eyes, and the fist-sized bee continues to attack me with mindless ferocity; I stand and walk (but only towards lighted areas, never the dark places, for fear tells me to avoid these if I value my continued stay on planet Earth) and tell myself that the two states of sleep and wakefulness are distinct from each other; but my sensible brain knows only confusion.

In sleep I talk. No random spurting of single words is this, but a whole, night-long conversation. On one legendary occasion, I began the night by asking my wife about the cost of an unnamed painting. She, being half asleep at the time, responded by admitting that she did not know. Later in the night I questioned her again, asking about the painting's origins. She did not say anything immediately, but apparently I persisted by pressing her with the question until she replied once again that that she knew nothing. The night continued in this manner until, at about six in the morning, I pressured her into responding to what was probably my tenth question. Her reply must have struck me as lacking enthusiasm because I confronted her with the accusation: - 'you are not interested in the painting, are you?' Being honest (and tired) she grunted 'No, I'm not interested in the rotten painting.' Whenever she recounts this episode, a gleam always enters her eye at this point as she readies herself to tells the final instalment, which consists of me turning to her and admitting: - 'No, I'm not interested in it either.'

If I am capable of sustaining a night-long conversation, then it is hardly surprising that the odd line or verse of poetry escapes from me and finds its way onto my computer. In general I understand what I write, but there are rare occasions where the poem SEEMS to make sense but I am incapable to deciphering its meaning. Perhaps if I read it while on the dream-side of the margin between my two worlds, the meaning will become clear.

(I am hoping that John will forgive my publishing a private email but the great poets always had their letters published PB :-)

SPYGLASS

just in case you thought I'd finished sending you stuff, here is one that is 100% Morphine written! I experience a particularly irritating side effect when I take the occasional glug of liquid morphine as opposed to my regular twice-daily doses of the pill variety. After taking the liquid, I sometimes find it impossible to distinguish between the real world of hard rocks and birds that fly and sheep that do not, and the altogether less predictable world of my imagination and dreams. Things happen when I am on the margin between the two - sheep DO fly, rocks become spongy (unless I fall on them) and beasties appear and disappear at will. A very odd place to be, especially at 3 in the morning! Worse still, Italk a lot... Sue generally wakes, but she fails to listen to my incoherent ramblings. This failing on her part causes me to lose most of the inspirational words I utter. Just once in a while, I remember the stupid things I've said in the between world, and even less frequently I manage to make sense of them the following day. Last night (we are finally getting to the point) I repeated a sentence a hundred times over a 4 hour period. The line was:- 'I desire me a spyglass to look to the future...' Such an antique name for the object; spyglasses are more generally known as telescopes; and how odd the phraseology - why insert the ME in the line? Very 18th century. There is no reason behind the line, but OTHER phrases and words occurred to me through the night - they can be discovered littering the attached poem SPYGLASS. What amazed me was the fact that I could type in all these meaningless snippets and end up with a complete poem containing a pertinent message.
Hope you like it.

John

Spyglass

I desire me a spyglass
To look far to the future,
To see what awaits me
Past Time's dull horizon;

And I desire me a compass
And a chart of the latest
To guide me fast forward
To the land where Fate wills me.

Yet I desire me a timepiece
That crawls through the minutes
And holds back the hours
'Tween this time and that;

And I desire me a slow sun
That idles and leisures,
That's reluctant to let
The moon take its throne.

Yet no compass nor spyglass
Nor slow sun or inching clock
Will alter by one jot
What awaits me at last.

Simply Three Words
A Triolet

The saying of those words
Is the music of my soul.
When:-‘I love you,’ she whispers,
The saying of those words
Is the rhythm of my life
And the basis of my future dreams.
The saying of those words
Is the music of my soul.

Aspiration

Think this when you think of me -
He is a principal poltergeist,
A ringleader of the amorphous clan,
And, though but a mortal man,
He once was apprentice to the playful ghosts
Whose time is spent in irritating jest.
Who would have guessed
That his capering ways were
Practise for the days
When his spirit alone remained?
Remember how he would hide your book,
And his look would give nothing away?
And recall the times his puppy humour
Would have you furious,
Yet he would beguile you with a grin.
And did you not, a thousand times,
Begin to knit, only to find
Your yarn tied in knots and
Ravelled round the legs of chairs
While he chanted from upstairs
'Knit one, purl one -
Is that jumper nearly done?'
Think now: 'He is famed as
Chief amongst the troupe of
Shoe-hiding, pan-dropping,
Noises-in-the-night
Invisible folk
Who have a joke at your expense.
And think 'Would I prefer him here
Where I can keep an eye on him,
Or is it better to leave him playing
In the love strings of my heart?'

Indebted

My life had travelled troubled highways,
Seldom finding placid water,
Yet you ever tower beside me
Seeding hope in me.

Each new place I lay my head down,
Every town I ever visit,
There I see your fearless spirit
Lifting me from grief.

All along the day's calm focus
I can feel your kind heart beating,
I can hear your soft voice rising
Clothing me in love.

Three Disconnected Poems

You'll remember that I've been having trouble with morphine and its effects - hallucinations, nightmares, mood swings and all the rest of it. well, for the first time late last week I had a GOOD reaction. I awoke in pain at one in the morning (this has become quite a habit) and went downstairs to have a top-up dose of liquid morphine. While I waited for it to kick in I armed myself with a notepad and a pencil. I wrote, or rather my HEAD did the writing for me. It was only some time later that I read back my words and realized that I had completed three disconnected poems that required only the most minor cosmetic changes before they could be called complete. My first idea was to lump them together under the heading 'Morphine Poems' but I have since decided to leave them as individual pieces. I have attached them all.

Liverpool and Mexico

I know a man in Mexico
Who will eat your pain –
And because pain is finite,
When he has it
You know pain not.
There is another man in Liverpool
Who devours your love –
And because love is likewise infinite,
There is none of your love
Remaining for me.

(ii)

Some Time Later

Hush now, it is calm now,
The sea has retreated
Exposing the sand to
The winds of the bay.

Shoals become islets
Drying in the sunlight,
Cruel reefs are the crags
Where the old women lay.

Long gone is the flood tide,
And the storm has passed over,
And save for the drowned man
What abided abides on.

(iii)

Relative Dimensions

If a pea is my heart
Then you are Australia,
And the moon is the size
Of the kiss that we share;
And if this galaxy represents
The breadth of our love,
Where are the universes
To correspond to our dreams?

Jungle

A leopard sits above me
In a rambling
Banyan tree;

A leopard waits above me
In a rambling
Banyan tree.

I ask forgiveness of the python,
But he slinks away
Whispering
No Siree.

A condor sweeps
Out of the hills
With meat upon its breath;

A condor sweeps
Down from the hills
With meat upon its breath.

A python and a condor
And a leopard –
Certain death.

Singing at the edge of dreams.

All through my troubled days
I see you,
Singing at the edge of dreams.
When the shadows threaten
And fear grows strong,
My shield is the love who never deserts me
Singing at the edge of dreams.
My control is slipping
And my sleep is troubled,
And my senses crumble away;
Yet when the black of night
Mets the grey of day,
I will hear you
Singing at the edge of dreams.

Question

Where the empty armchair sits,
There once sat you –
Quiet on your quiet days,
Or welling deep with energy
With an urge to share
Your endless joy with me.

That chair, bereft of you,
Is but a lifeless shade,
A gloomy, silent reminder
Of evenings in your company,
Of sweet hours and short days,
And of devotion.

Chairs do not experience love,
Nor do they know the loneliness
That separation brings.
Should I then feel more sorry for
The heartless furniture,
Or for the cheerless me?

Montage *(December Thoughts)*

i

She says she lives in a bubble.
It protects her,
Saves her from facing the truth
Every day.
Were she more of a poet,
She would liken her defence to
A wall of steel
Or a stone castle,
A knight with armour
Or a GI in a tank
Or a hackneyed ostrich
With its head in the proverbial sand.
Being her, she lives in her prosaic bubble
And feels no pain.
She pretends,
But her smiles are genuine.
If you value her happiness at all,
Do not burst her priceless bubble.

ii

For Christmas I will have
A book of short stories
And a 20 piece jigsaw
But no new clothes
Or jewellery
Or anything that will last
More than a few months.
Oh, I'd like a few nonsense items
From the Gadget shop
To amuse me,
And a mobile phone
To cover me
In emergencies.
But most of all,
For Christmas
I just want to
Be here
At Christmas.

iii

Say what you like,
Getting the blue badge for the car
In record time
(48 hours from application
To receipt)
May seem like a victory to you,
But for me
The public declaration
That I am disabled
By displaying the parking permit
Is one horrendous defeat.

iv
Flowers are blue and white
And orange and yellow
And a hundred other hues:
I wonder if they look
At their neighbours
And are prejudiced
Against those whose colour
Does not match their own.
I doubt it.

v
You can't take it with you!
Nope, so I'll spend it all right now,
And gather in my finance drawer
A stack of statements
Showing just how much I'm overdrawn.
If I can't take cash with me,
It's pretty damned certain
The bailiffs won't chase me
Where I'm going.

vi
Read my fortune, I dare you.
See how short the lines are?
Will you mention them when
The Tarot cards turn up
The dreaded pattern,
Or will you fudge and shirk
And pretend I have a future?
Whatever you say, I will laugh –
But not in your face.

vii

Huh! So you've got a cold, eh?
Maybe flu?
A snotty nose and a head like a drum?
Aching muscles and bones that creak?
Oh, have my sympathy,
Sincere and unreserved,
I lay it on by the shovelful;
But don't forget to
Sneeze in a direction other than mine.
I may love you
And feel sorry for you,
And be happy to make your tea,
But I object to
You blowing your germs
Anywhere near me.

viii

If you fast-forward over my first 17 years
And fast-forward again over the final year or so,
The video of my life is a romance,
A comedy, a manic Whitehall farce,
A series of miniature dramas
With a dash of pornography thrown in for balance.
I've got no complaints.

ix

You support me 95% of the time,
I support you 2% of the time;
The remaining 3% is a bonus.

Sweet, Sweet Day

Sweet, sweet day,
With the hazy sky as blue as an egg
Behind an airbrushed cloud,
And a breeze judged right to
Blow away the feathery mists
That gather over the fields.
Only an agile milkman and an
Early riser on a quiet bike
Disturb the muffled tranquillity,
But I welcome the dimension they add
To my solitary, reflective walk.

Dreamer

Smoke swirls from a cigarette's bright end
Sending signals in billowing clouds
That stain fairylight dust motes
Floating in a sunbeam's soft snare;

Stream rises from a coffee cup,
Scenting the room with its tempting aroma,
Becoming the ghost of the ghost
Of the poor man who died
Once he'd picked the beans for a penny a day;

Breath condenses in the outside,
In the ice world of winter,
Vying with the sky
And its snow-packed roof,
Yet ever failing to take form
Or become something more solid.

If all are transient,
As they are,
And all are shapeless and ever changing,
As they must be
As they will be,
And if all are momentary
And fleeting and gone in an instant,
This will not preclude them
From possessing the power
To tempt the idle dreamer,
To entice him to watch them,
To watch them and dream on.

A routine visit

She said 'how are you?' in the way doctors do. Six years of intensive training evidently isn't sufficient to arm them the word skills necessary to avoid this universal oil slick of inane rhetoric.

My intuitive yet unspoken response to that is always 'Bloody awful, otherwise I wouldn't be taking up you time or mine sitting in your dull surgery when I ought to be at home doing something useful.' But I generally find a fake smile from somewhere and utter an equally inconsequential 'Not too bad,' before adding, after a suitable pause when our eyes meet for the first time, 'except...'

On that day I had two 'excepts.'

'My ear's been giving me hell for about a week now,' I said, pointing to the place in question. 'Probably an infection. Nothing much, but I think a course of antibiotics might be in order.'

As she searched the papers and clutter of her drawers for the instrument she was looking for, I filled the silence by telling her about my other concern.

'My chest,' I said, again indicating the relevant area. 'I've had this cough for weeks now, on and off. I can't shift it, especially not in this weather.'

She extracted a grey plastic box from the jumble of the desk, opened it, checked the tiny light of the inspection tool by clicking the switch on and off three times, and peered into my ear, declaring a few seconds later, 'It looks clear. Perhaps a little redness, but I suspect that's nothing to worry about. You shouldn't use cotton buds to clean it.'

While checking my other ear for reasons known only to her, she asked, 'Do you smoke?'

'I used to,' I admitted. I wondered if she could feel the half smile of pride touching my mouth while her attention was taken up with the unaffected side of my head. Whatever you go to a doctor for – bad stomach, severe headache, dizziness and, I suspect, even an ingrowing toenail – they always enquire about your tobacco usage. On the rare occasions when I had previously found myself in this position, I tended to become almost apologetic, knowing that my habit offended the life view of the medical profession as a whole; but this time I had a defence. 'I've just quit,' I declared, lifting the sleeve of my tee-shirt to reveal the transparent oblong of plastic recognised by all as a nicotine patch. 'Three days ago.'

'How many did you smoke?'

Guiltily, I confessed, '40.'

Had she been a plumber or an electrician rather than a young, attractive GP with attractive Irish eyes, there would have been a momentous intake of breath at this juncture; instead, she looked at me with a meaningful frown.

'For how long?'

'Since I was a teenager. Maybe 40 years.' An exact calculation seemed pointless. What's a year or two either way at my age? 'But I've done with them now,' I bragged, and again I touched the patch before finishing, 'I've had enough of coughing.'

Then came the tactless, sharp, daisy-cutter, Hiroshima bombshell; she played the part of the guileless guillotiner with admirable proficiency.

'It could be lung cancer.'

Silence.

A silence lasting a year. Trees could have budded, flowered, grown as thick and tall as beanstalks, and lost their withering foliage beneath a fall of snow a metre deep in the interval between that utterance and the next.

How heavy can a hammer fall? How hard can a punch land? How painful can words be? Hard enough to take away my breath and make me want to lash out or run away.

Nobody says something like that, not unless it is accompanied by a dismissive nudge or with a broad smile. Her statement was deadpan, businesslike, without passion.

There were other words, but they vanished before I could make sense of them. Seconds or minutes later, she pressed a rectangular rubber stamp on a small sheet of paper.

'We'd better get you down for a chest x-ray.'
'When?' I was now back on familiar ground. In my experience, all things medical involved long explanations repeated over and over again to people who seemed not to listen, appointments at the most inconvenient times, the twiddling of thumbs for hours in dire waiting rooms, and a long delay before results that frequently revealed nothing were received.
She replaced the instrument in her drawer and said 'Just go along to the hospital and they'll do it immediately.'
Immediately? Nothing is done immediately by the NHS unless it involves heart attacks or strokes... or a suspected cancer.

Outside The Map Room

A man and immortal,
Yet suddenly Death's portal
Gaped wide and inviting before me.

A sign overhead
Unarguably read
'Today you shall not ignore me.'

I took one tiny stride
To the door tall and wide
And saw there, laid out before me,

The future's fine map
That through chance or mishap
Marked out the way forward for me.

I shook off the coil
Of my body disloyal
To join the immortals before me,

And with one final leap
I plunge into the deep
(Please keep your fingers crossed for me!)

Counting Days

Logic told me to count myself unlucky when
They said my days were numbered.
Listen:
Numbered days are better than no days at all,
And luck is just being here
When so many have gone away.
Open a newspaper any day
And read the story beneath the headline:
'Youths in fatal car smash.'
Listen:
Their years were less than mine,
Their luck was all bad.
Logic says I should feel distressed,
Dismayed, distraught,
Anxious, uneasy,
Suicidal.
Listen:
Listen to my contrary view:
I am grateful,
Indebted, exhilarated,
Ecstatic,
For my numbered days
Are days to be celebrated,
And reason tells me
That counting them is
Something I will not do.

Whimsy

There are two of us in this dream.
I am Character Central, without a name,
No face, no shape, no frame;
Nothing an outsider could identify,
But I know that it is 'I'.

And then there is you,
With a face as clear as a photograph,
And youth on your side
Borrowed from twenty years ago –
I listen: you speak:

'For you, I will do,'
You say, adding nothing more.
I know what you mean
Because reading the unsaid is
Achievable in dreams.

I say, 'Take it away,'
Believing you will understand;
But all you do is laugh,
And you are undressed,
Diametrically wrong in your guess.

Take it away,' I repeat,
And you greet my plea
With a vanishing act;
And in this sleep I am alone,
Afraid dreams can become reality.

about Whimsy...

a deliberately inappropriate title for a piece that reflects one of the worst nights of my entire life. I was wide awake, standing up and drinking a glass of water alone in a cold, echoing dining room when this horrible 'vision' came into my head. It is only love and dedication that keeps me alive; the prospect of that love being withdrawn for

Weapons Inadequate (Light)

Light, but insufficient
Despite the multitude of industrious bulbs
In adjacent rooms;

Deep, black, muffled darkness,
With a rumour under and behind,
Waiting with evil intent;

Light, but lacking muscle to depose the fear
Connecting this flesh to a different plane;

Terrifying shadows, as heavy as lead,
As swift as dragonflies;

Light, but weaker than a starving mouse;
Dark, with octopus arms;

The shades occupy corners,
Dive out suddenly, unexpected,
Speak in tongues ancient yet familiar;

Light, silent, impotent;
Shadows imply intention.

A moment of defeat –
Ectoplasm arms reach out,
Touching nothing possessing a name,

Converging deeper than skin or bone;
They clasp the core,

Digging claws in.

Light at last has a voice
Articulating through the veil,
Saying 'a dream;

Nothing but a dream;'
And the chasing sound is believed
As the shadows retreat.

But an imbedded barb remains,
As black as fear.

Light, but too little of it;
An army stripped of swords.

***

LIGHT - again, this happened at 2 in the morning. The frightening part of it probably lasted 20 seconds before help appeared on the scene, but it could have been 10 years. What would I do without that support?

Empty

When,
Sun-baked to the colour
Of Mediterranean envy
And dirt smeared from his pathless
Wanderings in woodlands,
The boy returned home
With his heart set on comforts,
With his mind filled with soft chairs
And stew with great dumplings;
But
The house lacked the light
That announced people in it,
And the door was shut tight
With no key to be found.
He knocked at the door,
But his knock found no answer –
The sole sound to be heard
Was the drop of a tear.

Prologue to The Morphine Dream

Having reduced my morphine input last week on the recommendation of the doctor, I've been forced to up it by 25% again. The unavoidable result of this was a night of very disturbed sleep with a selection of peculiar thoughts drifting through my fogged brain. I have attached a poem (The Morphine Dream) which came to me in exactly the form you see here, including the definitive title. I have also attached a 750-word prose piece (Beyond the dream) describing the drama that followed.

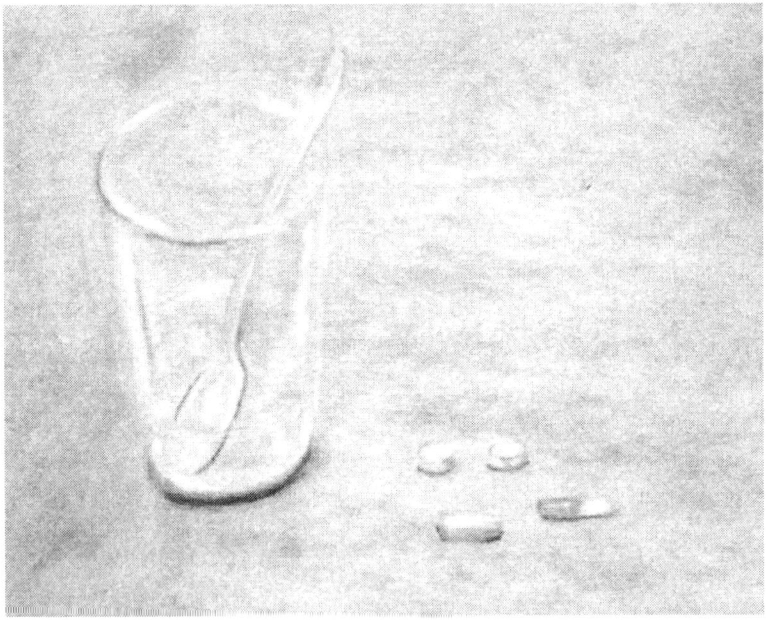

The Morphine Dream

Lazing
On a riverbank
In summer.
Blue sky;
Mind vacant
While the
Serpents
Gather round.

Beyond The Dream

Immediately after composing the poem 'The Morphine Dream' during a period of troubled sleep on the night of 16th January 2004, I witnessed this vivid scene:-

Unseen forces caused a young, strong man to lie, face up, on a massive, scrubbed-pine farmhouse table. The handsome man was dressed after the manor of a tough-but lovable Hollywood rogue in a puffed white shirt and tight breeches; his long, brown hair hung in a broad pony tail, and his sharp blue eyes stared directly at me, as if attempting to convey a message. If that was his intention, I lacked the wit to understand what the message might be.

It was evident that whoever or whatever bade him lay there had the means to secure him tightly because not once throughout the events that followed did he struggle or make the least attempt to escape.

Seconds passed and nothing in the room altered. I could see him and the table very clearly despite the gloom pervading the room, and all around were placed the accoutrements of a rude, rural life of the 17th or 18th century. Solid wooden beams held up a low roof, and from the beams hung a hunting gun almost as long as a man is tall; elsewhere perhaps four or five rabbits and pheasants swung slowly from metal hooks; copper cooking pans picked up the light from an open log fire and threw it back into the room with a feint, golden glow; and an island of drying washing hung like lifeless sails before the small, square window set into the wall opposite me. It all seemed perfectly ordinary. Such charmingly recreated rustic rooms can be seen almost every day of the week in folk museums scattered up and down the country.

Suddenly the man's eyes began to blink rapidly but irregularly, somehow indicating to me that pain and fear together had set their chill hands upon him. Without a sound being made, his neck slowly thickened and stretched. His jaw, neck and the top part of his muscular chest became one single, repulsive alien object, littered with sinew and veins that throbbed beneath the pale, taut skin. This preternatural mass grew inch by inch, enlarged and extended by an incomprehensibly strong, unassailable force until it was twice as long as the rest of his body. I had a presentiment that something even more awful than this unnatural growth waited the man. In the Morse of his flickering eyes he intimated to me that I should look up towards the dusty beams, and I, having by this time become convinced that his destiny and mine were linked and that I possessed the power to prevent his demise, obeyed. There, suspended between the gun and the corpses of the dull-eyed, recently murdered country animals, was the blade of a large, bright, deadly guillotine. There was no doubting its sharpness or purpose. Nothing held the blade in place. There was no rough, wooden scaffold around it, no rope or wire above it preventing its fall, and no platform or traditional bloodied wicker basket beneath it where the victim's head would land. The lack of these obvious trappings meant that there would be no execution, meant that the blade would not fall onto the wide target of his abnormal neck, and meant that the symbol of Parisian Terror could not, therefore, be the agent of his death.

Could not, that is, unless his mind declared that it could.

This was a familiar feeling: the inevitable becomes the impossible if one has the determination to make it so. All I need do was communicate my understanding to him – to tell him that the blade was a harmless piece of metal that, in all likelihood, did not exist in reality – and he would survive. 'Stop believing in it,' was all I need say. 'Tell it to go and it will be gone.'

But the evil, unseen forces waited in the shadows, thirsty for a victim. If the man on the table escaped his bloody fate, the invisible entities would look in my direction.

My voice remained still.

I said nothing.

The blade came down.

I looked away.

John J Whitmarsh
18th January 2004

Prelude to Inscription...

Things occur that demand a change of plan. I began the day (at 6.00 AM) with every intention of sifting through my emails to find amusing and/or informative fragments for use on the remaining pages of my morphine book. My waking time being some two hours before Sue's, I idled away the intervening period thinking, reading and listening to Tchaikovsky on the radio because I could not get to the computer while she was in bed. As she staggered into the living room, I offered to make her a cup of tea. She muttered 'yes, please,' and I put the kettle on. Several minutes later, a mug of tea appeared in my hand – she had completed the task of tea-making because I had, by then, become distracted by a scientific magazine! While supping, she confirmed that the new pills had given me a restful night's sleep, marred only by a single incident. I asked her to explain, and she said: - 'you sat up, recited a poem... whole, complete, finished, new.... And then, as you spoke the last line, you lay down again and began to snore.'

I can assure you that such experiences are not uncommon in Castle Whitmarsh.

She then went on to tell me that she, being wide awake at the time of the impromptu open mic session, had made a determined effort to remember the poem word for word by repeatedly reciting it to herself.

Inscription One

In a graveyard
There's a gravestone.
The gravestone is inscribed
With a woman's name;
And also the names of
Mary, Jane and George,
Alice and Bill,
Kath and James,
Pearl and Tim and Sally,
And Mum and Dad,
And Margaret, Pauline and Magenta,
And Peter and David and Jim.

Some of these are no longer living,
Some have moved on,
And some still remember.
But there's a gravestone
Inscribed with a woman's name,
And the message repeats
Over and over:-
Rest in peace, rest in peace,
Rest in peace.

Inscription Two

In a graveyard where damp moss has taken hold,
Where the cold wind cuts
All but the stoutest hearts to tears,
Where bowed and weeping trees have made their home
And where silent owls search by sound alone
In the stillness of the night,
Stands an ancient gravestone of black and polished granite;
And inscribed upon it
Is the name of the woman there interred,
And all around her hallowed name,
Chiselled with rare craft almost forgotten in this
Our computer aided age,
Chiselled with letters crisp and deep,
But not as deep as the grave's
Mourned and much loved tenant,
Are the names of the mass of distraught well-wishers
Who offered up a sacrificial coin
To have the stone erected in her honour.
The identities of these undemanding benefactors
Are plain for all to see:-
Pearl and Sally and Tim,
Kath and James,
Alice and Bill,
And Peter and David and Jim;
Margaret and Pauline
And Mum and dad,
And Magenta and Mary,
And Jane and George
And all the friends
The woman ever had.

In a graveyard, dour and dank,
Where the past clings tenaciously on
And the present is but an uninvited guest

With little to encourage a lengthy stay,
There stands a stone
With this message chiselled deep
For the one singled out as
Too soon gone,
So long gone:-

Rest in Peace –
We, your comrades, your lovers, your family,
Your damp cheeked supporters who will miss you
More than the air we breathe,
Wish and implore you, our cherished one, to
Rest in Peace.

Rest in Peace eternal,
Taking for your cue
Our etched, indelible names,
And from this stone
Sturdy and invincible,
And from the prayers
In our hearts to your omniscient keeper,
Omnipotent yet invisible.

Rest in Peace, the woman who lies here,
Though some of us lay dead alongside you,
And others who have time ahead
To mourn your memory and await the day
When they, too, are slipped into the mother earth
To rest in peace beneath a headstone who's true worth
Is measured not in granite
But in the words inscribed upon it.

SOME E-MAIL EXTRACTS

Me? I'm that little, (sometimes pleasant) guy who lives inside the big, tough guy who, in turn, resides in the body of a little weak guy who inhabits the form of the street-fighting, knife-carrying, woman-hating (and loving) lout who found refuge inside a poet whose only bad habits are smoking, looking at (but not touching) anything vaguely female that happens past. As for you, I think the outer you is more or less real... no matter how hard I look, I can see nothing suggesting that a WORSE you resides anywhere. It must be nice to be so uncomplicated. Your kids love you, a man WOULD love you if you gave him the opportunity, and all your friends adore you. What you see is what you get, and people appreciate that in you. I lost track of who the REAL me was years ago. I don't think I'd like to find out!

..........Thoughts go skittering around my head...

I have a friend who is an Indian... a Hindu. His culture goes in for arranged marriages. He tells me that love is much purer if it grows from friendship and respect rather than if it were rooted in lust (as is the western custom!) Since his marriage has lasted as long as mine and both he and his wife are devoted to each other, I can't really argue! Maybe that is why you and your husband did so well together.

... another skitter... all life is balanced on very fine points! I call them pivotal points. My marriage came about because I happened, for the one and only time in my life, to walk back from a football match rather than getting the bus (1967 - Crystal Palace FC, their ground was situated in Croydon, where I lived.) SHE went to a fee-paying school and it just so happened that on this one and only Saturday she had to attend school to take part in a rehearsal for a drama. Yours truly, elated because his team had won a rare match, spied her as she walked in the opposite direction on the far side of the road. I dodged traffic and threw my arms around the girl who was a complete stranger to me, and said I wanted to fall in love with her! She told me to pee off (err.. no... the school she went to was VERY posh... she actually said something akin to 'unhand me, foul varmint!) I protested, telling her that I knew her and that her memory was at fault if she did not recognise me. She responded with a furious 'what's my name then?' I guessed - plucking a relatively common name from mid-air. 'Susan' I said. My lucky (Fate-inspired?) guess held her attention just long enough for me to get her phone number... which I wrote down on the back of a match box in the red gunk that you get if you lick the live end of a match! Neither of us had a pen - thank heavens for Bryant and May!... and the rest is run-of-the-mill romance. Ten seconds later, or any other deviation from the timetable or logistics of the day, and we would not have met! Fate? Chance? Or just one of a series of possible outcomes?..........

Despite all you say, I still contend that my ideal woman can be summed up quite briefly in this statement:-

'Wear clothes that I would not dream of wearing (thus jeans, tee-shirts and trainers are definitely out), have your hair cut in a style I would not be dare go out in, and hold a conversation without swearing at least once in each sentence. If you do that, admirers will throw themselves at you.

Good Sue/ Bad Sue

Alan Corkish, a dear friend, recently sent an email to me suggesting that he had written amorous letters to my wife. The following is an extract of my reply >>>

I mentioned your comment about love letters from you to Sue, my beloved... and she replied that she would be as dilatory responding to letters proclaiming undying devotion as she is to the host of emails that currently reside unread and unanswered in her Outlook inbox. Even her very best friends – with whom she has recently become reunited thanks to the aptly named 'friends reunited' website – have to wait a month or more before she finds the time or inclination to sit her bum on the swivel chair and clack out a letter.

(1) At the very top of the list of her prospective future soulmate's list of virtues would have to be patience by the ton.

That quality, she insists, would need to be balanced exactly by all of the following:

(2) An interesting personality with plenty to say, but prepared to accept her soap-boxed views as gospel;

(3) Wealth without limit;

(4) A hatred of pet animals;

(5) A willingness to dust, wash up, Hoover, make beds, iron, tidy and generally take care of 90% of all household tasks;

(6) A detestation of right-wing attitudes, alcohol, nicotine, gambling, religion and all other addictive substances;

(7) A determination to share all wealth with her in any way that she sees fit;

(8) A complete and utter lack of emotional baggage, ex-wives, children, history or previous life;

(9) A desire to indulge in sex only once every two weeks, and then strictly on her terms;

(10) A promise that he (the candidate for her heart) will swiftly be overtaken by a grievous illness guaranteed to lead to his demise the moment a suitable will has been drawn up and

signed;

(11) And finally the most important qualities of all – that he should be devoted to her despite her cold, harsh treatment of him through out the term of their bonding.

I think she will put an advert in the S & M gazette reading: rich, willing slave wanted – must be interesting, solvent, etc. NO WIMPS.

Sue read the above, frowned, accused me of blackening her character in front of a prospective admirer, and demanded that I publish a list of her GOOD points. In the meantime, Alan said – rather dishonestly, I suspect – that he would fail to meet Sue's demands on one single point.

I write the following to Alan, allowing Sue to read it before I hit the 'SEND' button.

Fail on ONE of Sue's points?? Any self-respecting chauvinist should fail on them all… I celebrate the fact that I do! Sue was miffed when I mentioned my good-humoured revelation of her self-centred wish-list, and she tells me that I must behave myself in future; so to put the record straight, I will list her good points:-

(1) She is the perfect slave for any man prepared to put her in her place

(2) She devotes herself 100% to the object of her love

(3) She is intelligent, animated, malleable, physically fit, has all her own teeth and hardly has any difficulty whatsoever hearing

(4) She will soon fall into that most desirable category of 'rich widow' if, as I do, you consider owning her own house and car, and having 75 grand in the bank sufficient capital to elevate her into that class

(5) She has no bad habits whatsoever. Doesn't drink, smoke, gamble, use drugs of any description, or hold any religious beliefs

(6) She has been taught to accept communism and the far left as the optimum form of government, but is willing to accept a lesser form of socialism. She will ALWAYS use her vote, if only to keep out the worst of the bunch

(7) She loves children, hates dogs, loves travel and adventure, hates boredom, spends £20 more a week than she receives, detests the art of saving money.

(8) She is nice – add that only because it is how she would describe herself.

(9) She can cook well, provided simple, basic cooking without a list of ingredients as long as your arm is to your taste. Detests curry, loves pasta and salad

(10) She looks 10 years younger than her age

(11) She always smiles, and is the perfect partner at a social gathering because she makes friends exceedingly quickly AND she possesses the skill to remember their names

(12) She has had only one careful owner

Right, I think she'll be satisfied with that lot...

Thanks to Alan Corkish for allowing me to use this item.

Upon receiving a grant for an automatic bed

Sometimes real life is far too complicated and confused to seem real. If I decided to write the BED saga as a fiction, I would immediately be slapped round the ear and told to go away and stop writing such nonsense. Yesterday SHOULD have been pretty straightforward... all the guy needed to do was put on 4 legs or one new strut. He arrived, discovered that he still had two legs that were unsuitable, but gamely changed all the fittings (it took over an hour) until it all worked. BUT he had arrived without the requisite castors!! To get them, he had to drive all the way to a warehouse in Manchester (an hour each way over the Pennines), but he heroically returned with them in his paws, tried them, swore ever so quietly, and confessed that the castors were perfect, but that they too had been supplied with wrong fittings!! By this time, Sir John was growling in quite a threatening manner. The man vanished into his van, made a call on his mobile, and announced that he was off to Manchester again. Two hours later he returned, used his hammer and screwdriver for a total of ten seconds, and declared that everything was in order! Almost guiltily, I suggested that the time had come to try out the motor. He went white, requested a cup of tea and while I was downstairs, he fiddled in silence. By the time the kettle was boiling, he shouted 'it works!' in the way an excited child might!! After he had gone, I lay there, playing with my remote until it almost melted, and wondering why it took 8 weeks to get to this stage!! But eventually a good night's sleep was had by all (interrupted at around 3 in the morning, but I refuse to tell you why because my wife would get very embarrassed!!)

Reflections or Confessions
A fragment

Sat by a sun-shocked window with a keyboard perched
lazily on my lap,
I laze back, hoping to reflect upon my life in the way rays
From the sun reflect off the rich, red glass container resting
on the table beside me –
a glass designed as a receptacle for sickly sweet, lava hot,
Alien yet so English apple tea,
But employed only as the gathering place for
Drifting motes, and left there, dustily, dryly
And decorously for the soothing notes it brings to the
Otherwise cluttered room in which I squander
My last, long, leisured, stressed, sleep-lost, stay-wake-at-
night
And slumber the afternoon away days.
My senses insist I am a prisoner of time,
Locked up and with the keys thrown away
And bars thicker than Big Ben to keep me in,
But instinct begs me go again, go and revisit
The places where experience was gained
Look again at the faces that shaped me,
Read again from the library of my memory
The thousand books where philosophy
And life were found, and step again
Upon the ground that seemed so solid once upon a time.
Once upon that time, I discovered dockweeds
To take away the nettle's sting; once,
I sat beneath a wide and mighty canopy
And listened to the melodic trill and exciting shrill
Of birds, and learned their names one by one,
Putting words to their songs, chanting:-

'A little bit of bread and NO cheese',
And smugging inwardly as I had another tag
To add to the swelling list. Once,
I could not resist the call of the wild,
The cry to the starving child that promised
Nature's bounty in one of London's pleasanter Home
Counties.
'Sanctuary' said the sign, and I read it as mine!
I sought, not altogether in vain,
For the meaning of the clause
'Trespassers will be prosecuted' –
For if by 'prosecuted' the writer had intended the words
To portray a fleeing child with shotgun pellets
Drizzling down in a threatening cloudburst behind him,
And supposed the scene to switch, some moments later
To the house where a pair of shorts ripped
And rent upon the barbed wire of a high,
Snapping fence were put on display to an angry,
Snapping mother who despaired of ever paying off
Her loans to the draper and greengrocer,
Then he composed the sign well.
The shorts were sewn, grotesquely,
As a lesson in humiliation not to be forgotten in a hurry,
And the worry ever after was that others would have
memories
As cutting-clear as mine. In the unravelling of jumpers'
threads,
Caught on the barbs of brambles,
Or snagged on branches high up in conker trees
Where money could be earned from townies whose ability
To shake brown gold from the leaves was not half as good
as mine,
Came the unravelling of money-making plans,

For every penny hard earned and sweated for
Was spilled out under pressure from a torturing tongue
And laid on the table in readiness to pay for the wool
required.
I recall the cry: - 'It's tan – not a colour I have in,
And by the hank it costs more than I can make in half a day.
Someone has to pay, and the jumper's owner
And the fault and the cause of all this ruckus is nobody but
you.'
It seemed both harsh and fair,
Nor would I dare argue that the Beano and gobstopper
I had my heart set upon were far better value
Than a stretch of wool to darn the jumble sale rag
That I could manage without and had never liked
Since the day she brought it home
Along with the coat that never fitted.

Brief Reflections on Marriage

I married a woman called Mrs No
Which was something of a bitter blow;

But then she fell ill and died, God Bless,
And I found for myself a Mrs. Yes.

Ballad of a Needlephobe

Starting now in ballad mode
I will describe my lengthy narrative,
And recount to you the brute conduct
Of one nurse, and what she did.

She stood across the room from me,
Fearsome needle in her hand,
And waved proud her steely weaponry
As bid me bravely stand.

'No pain will come of it,' she swore,
And, sooth, I swore by return,
For needles with their glinting points
My fullest loathing earn.

'I pray to you, Oh nurse in blue,'
If you care for me this day,
Deliver true your trusty drugs
In some other, point-free way.'

I petitioned her for tablets
Or for sweet pills by the score,
And as I pleaded with the brutish nurse
I eyed the shut but haven door.

'There is no other way,' she held,
'To deal with your disease;
Come, let me prick you just this once.'
Oh! the trembling of my knees.

'I implore you, please, absent that steel,

That javelin in disguise,'
My fear, I rue, stole all my strength
And summoned water to my eyes.

She strode with steps a mile long
To stand high by my side,
And said the pain would soon be gone,
'Struth, t'will will never start!' I cried.

I ripped the devilish implement
From her sturdy clutch
And threw it clear across the room,
But she pained me in the crutch.

I fell a-wailing to the ground,
Groaning sharp and shrill;
The she flung herself upon the tool
And moved in for the kill.

All my strength I called upon,
And my manly courage swelled;
It had come to this, a battle,
'Twixt me and all the world.

I lashed fair hard with fists and feet,
As her banshee screams let out;
Ah, I fought the battle of my life,
Gaining victory from the rout.

The nurse with the accursed needle
Lay lifeless in the room;
I marched in glee from the field of war,
Mindless of my doom.

For in that fight, that battle wild,
That I won with determination,
I forgot that Death would claim me quick
If denied my healing medication.

I lay me here on my dying bed
Alone, racked with my infection;
Ah, life would last four-and-twenty years longer
If I had braved but one injection.

When Death shows me his lair of flame,
Oh, in Hades' fire's reflection,
I will spy my private Hell's dire form
An eternity's injection!

Porcelain Cup

An emperor came to visit me.
One Mikado, dressed in all the very best,
With shoulders wider than a door,
Wider than the portal to any mortal realm,
And with skirts billowing like sails from a mighty warship,
Came to visit me.
He sat upon my settee,
Proud, conceited, vain
(And with cause to be vain),
And he was Opera Fantastic dramatic.

He took up a biscuit from the saucer
Which held the porcelain cup
And broke off one quarter and began,
With the long nail of his royal right hand,
To etch the likeness of Beijing in the chocolate covering
Of that quartered impressive digestive.
We saw, yet we did not like to say
(We feared the outcome if we did dare say)
That his attempts at art were,
For all his regal splendour,
Incontrovertibly poor!
And then he strode with steps a nation wide
To my computer and typed
(In letters as bold as Attila
Or the most Genghist Khan of all)
The boastful name Beijing.
It is in capitals, I declared.
Yes, decreed he, For Beijing
Is a capital,
And must be writ as such!

Non syllable

Who spoke the word?
Whose intellect shaped it,
Mapped it
And sent it through the air,
Allowing me to hear?

It has no meaning, this word;
It possesses neither consonants nor vowels,
Has no syllables, no stress,
Has no emphasis at front or rear;
Yet someone spoke it to my ear
And said it bold and sharp and clear.

That word –
Formless, unrepeatable,
Without structure or sound –
Originated from lips and larynx,
Was created by an entity
With intellect and will,
And was aimed directly at me in the
Turmoil of my night.

That word,
It entered my mind,
Lodged there, sent synapses reeling
With its urgency;
But I cannot fathom it,
Cannot unravel it.
No hide nor hair of it makes sense,
But yet
It does not diminish,

Its echo goes on and on,
No softer, no louder.

Said once and never again,
That word remains inside me,
Haunting, occupying my attention;
But it has no more shape or meaning
Than the creak of a house settling
Down to rest after a common,
Frantic day.

That word –
Who spoke it,
Whose lips and intelligence
Gave vent
To that one, amorphous word?

Between two worlds

No tiger tail or aniseed,
No frangipani or dancing weed,
No Northern lights or whippoorwills,
No goblins grim or whisky stills;
Nothing much bizarre around,
But every step upon Dream's ground
Is taken with cold trepidation
For in this daydream, nightdream nation
Nothing is as it should be
Except for me and the walking tree.

Hush

There will be no bells for me,
No loud lament,
No celebration of a body failed and collapsed,
No pretence of resurrection,
Nor any casket of oak or finest elm
To shield my shoddy remains
From the rampant jaws of worms.

Never will I be interred with high ceremony
In the iron earth
To begin a second journey
With a triumphant fanfare
Louder than the first.

I arrived free from publicity,
With an unheard wail
And a gasp –
And so will be my last.
When the forecast moment comes,
I will choose the hearth,
And let my ashes be carried away
In a plastic bag,
And the world shall be no wiser
Of my departure
Than it was of my unsung birth.

But this there will be –
A memory of me
In heads that value
Thoughtful silence above
The measly price of an
Easy granite
Obituary.

Breakers

**Breakers breaking hard against the hard rock,
Splintering,
Glistening in the sunlight;
Knife-sharp and cool,
Like an assassin on assignment,
Cutting the air
With the silence of wire.**

More Musings

........Just to say thanks for your concern... I think I tend to panic sometimes, imagining the worst. My "nurse" is learning how best to relieve the peaks of my pain through massage, and although she has the touch of an elephant, it does help a little. I've been suffering from nausea for several days, but I think I've finally tracked down the cause... too many cups of tea! For some reason, it reacts with the increased doses of Morphine. As simple as that! So the solution is to cut down my intake by half. Since doing that, the Morphine SEEMS to be more effective, and I've managed two nights of restful sleep on the trot.............

I am alternating between multitasking like a maniac and falling asleep at the keyboard. The new pills (damn them) have turned me into a manic/somnambulist! The doc says I'll get used to them shortly and my levels will adjust properly, but at the moment I'm like a car with six gears that only operates in TOP or NEUTRAL.

My drugs situation has changed. They are reducing my intake of morphine slightly and substituting the shortfall with a new animal that does away with the 'dreams', but which causes me to sleep 8 hours a night plus three hours in the day! Naturally the pain is less, because I have fewer conscious hours in which to feel it; but when you take into account the fact that I am presently on one-third of the eventual dose (it increases in three-day steps and the morphine decreases likewise until I am on one-half the original dose) I should sleep for 24 hours a day, all of which will be completely pain free! Umm... either their logic or mine is up the spout!

and a quotation....(the context of which, shall remain anonymous!)
........I suspect she would argue the existence of oxygen and turnips if the mood took her!

Extract from an Email

I have told you a little about the strange inner-cranial happenings that often accompany an ingestion of liquid morphine. Last night I came out with two modern classics that Sue (my long-suffering spouse) noted down lest she forget:-
For reasons that I will never know, my mind drifted to the subject of lifts and who invented them. I said to Sue that I knew who the joint inventors of the contraption were. They were a pair of Americans (who called the machines 'elevators') by the names of Doctor T. Bey and City Tom. She asked how I reached that conclusion, and I sang her the logical reply: 'City Tom and Doctor T Bey.'
Explanation: many years ago Otis Redding sang 'Sitting on the Dock of the Bay.' Go into almost any lift and you will see that the name 'Otis' is placed on a legend plate riveted to the wall.... It seemed to make sense at the time!
And after that my mind sped on to a Bruce Willis movie 'Die Hard.' I asked my long suffering missis how one (anyone) could guarantee that they could die hard. She shook her head I expect and waited for me to shed some light on the matter. 'Easy,' I said. 'Your very last action should be to throw yourself into a sea of tranquil water beyond a river delta. That way, if nothing untoward happens, sediments will gently and slowly build up over you and, given a million years or so, you will become a fossil. When you are unearthed from the now solid rock by a palaeontologist in that future age, he will rightly be able to say "there is a woman who knew how to die hard!"'
Ummm... and I followed that up by referring to the second Willis film in the sequence. 'And do you know how to 'Die Hard Two?' 'No,' responded my wife (probably.) 'Easy,' I said. ''You instruct me to take my place in the sediment first, and then you follow.' Questions may have emerged from her lip at this time, but if they did, John was not listening. 'That way, when the palaeontologist digs us up, he will say that I knew how to die hard, and YOU knew how to 'Die Hard Too.'

Ho hum. SO logical when I am in a mixed world of reality and sleep!

On Timewasting

Upon passing the link to John for an online game where a Yeti-type creature baseball-bats a penguin across the snow, sliding on his belly towards the distance markers for the score......

Hi,
oh evil provider of asinine drivel, A plague and a pox be on thee for diverting mine energies away from the serious - nay, quasi-religious - business of serious versifying. How am I, a hapless, decrepit soul, supposed to produce world-shatteringly fabulous poetic marvels when my few remaining precious moments in this dominion are stolen from me to guide a Neanderthal towards a penguinous world record? Thou, O heinous creature, hath ruined the little commitment left in me, and led me to troubled waters. I trust that the fires of Hell will await thee as reward for thine evil act.
Yours in turmoil (and still without a champion score)
John The Baseball addict

As you know (and some of you know it a lot better than others) I have huge fun when I exceed the limits of my lovely painkilling morphine. Sometimes the results are frightening, sometimes they are amusing, sometimes they are peculiar and sometimes they are a mix of all the above. Earlier this week I found it necessary to boost my morphine intake at midday (not a rare occurrence), and I fell into a dreamless sleep. Some while later I THOUGHT I awoke to the real world. But that world was weird. The half to one side of me was perfectly normal, but the other half was non-existent. Imagine looking at you computer monitor as you are doing now, and being able to see only half the screen and half the keyboard and half of the desk upon which the computer sits. To bring the whole of the screen into focus, you would have to turn your head a long way to one side. Please TRY to imagine it.

Right – that sets the mood. Now read opposite, then turn the page.

Cyclopes Is Alive

Waking from a deep, timeless-as-death
Morphine sleep, I see a darkness there
In front of me. One side of my world
Is bright, illuminated by a flickering TV screen,
But the other is darker than the ocean's bed,
More impenetrable than a cocaine fable,
As black as your lonely bed-sit depression.
I analyse, decipher, contemplate;
Man - one of my eyes is missing.
The right one, I think.
I check, and yes, I have full use of the left.

But she is here – too close to fool,
Too alert in her ministry
For me to be able to kid.
I tell her to go on some fool's errand,
To brew tea for the pseudo-thirsty me,
Then I slide a disobedient foot over
The ground in front of me.
Carpet resists, but I insist
That every inch much be explored
Before she comes back through the door.
No eye there! Nothing at all
Save for the stool I use to
Store my earthly possessions.

I check visually with my good eye
(With my only eye). I am no Cyclops,
No harpie content to share eyes,
No one-eyed man in the kingdom of the blind;
My history has me bifocal,

But my present has me half-blind,
Half a man, an ocular cripple
With vision that must limp from
Scene to scene,
Leaving half the world unseen.

There is nothing! No round and rolling eye,
No marble-in-the-playground sphere
(I must be careful not to squash it!)

She returns.
She suspects.
She detects.
She says:-
'What's missing?' in a very casual way.
I reply:-
'My eye,' as if nothing odd was happening.
She smiles (on my good side)
And tells me that both of them are there:-
'Where?'
In your head where they ought to be,'
She giggles.
She smiles.
I agree with her, but I test it out surreptitiously,
Closing first one eye then the next,
Covering each in turn to check;
And they are there
(Or they appear to be).
Assured (or convinced
Just enough to close the both of them)
I sleep.
Seconds later (she says those seconds,
But I swear hours rolled by

In the playground of my head)
I awake again,
And she relates the story of my eye.
I laugh (or pretend to)
But check just one more time
That I am whole again.

She walks off to finish where
She left off making the tea,
And while she is away I feel
(Just once more)
Beneath the chair
In case
An eye is there.
But I find only a Malteeser
And last week's TV Times.

Work in progress - JJW

It may seem funny. It may seem odd. My problem is that it seems so bloody REAL when things like this happen! Before I went to bed that night (about 10 hours after the incident) I looked closely into the bathroom mirror just to check that both eyes were in place. Thankfully, they were!

The poem took me about 30 minutes to type (one handed, for reasons that are too boring to go into right now) but it has been growing in my head ever since the time in question. I think it could probably do with a little work before it is finished, and that is why my name does not appear at the foot of it. However, time is not my friend. I would hate to think that this snippet of life within the walls of Castle Whitmarsh would be seen by nobody. I seldom distribute work in progress items, so you may consider yourselves fortunate (or unfortunate) for being the ones to read it.

Much love

And a little bit of quite lightweight insanity

John

Final Promise

Minutes only remain, my love,
For me to express the way I feel,
For me to open up my heart to you
As I have never done before.
The door awaits for me, my love,
And soon I must be gone;
But before I do I must reveal
The welling of my soul.
You remove from me the pain of life
And take my fear away,
And every day I venture on
You mean much more to me.
No man has known a love like this,
Nor had a woman like you –
And before I go, hear this, my love,
Our love will reign beyond this realm.

Interesting Times

Ah, the freedom!
That which is
May change;
That which will be
Perhaps may not be;
Promises are merely
Empty suggestions,
And empty suggestions
May be made of concrete
Or of clay
Depending on the mood
Of the day.

Ah, the freedom!
If I suspect that
The pain monster
Is waiting over the hill
Or round the corner,
All I need do is wrestle with
The childproof top of a bottle
And consume the contents
Willy nilly.
The results –
Hallucinations,
Vomiting, dizziness
And the like
– are far more interesting than
Plain old pain.
Ah, the freedom
Of decision!

Alan Corkish & John J Whitmarsh

They come for me.

They hold shackles,
Have no keys,
Carry handcuffs,
With no keys for these;
Keys are surplus
There is no undoing
Of the chains
That will hold me.
My sentence
Has been considered
Its duration
Calculated.
In the darkness
Of that doorway
They hold shackles
Meant for me;
I cannot avoid them
Though I struggle,
Though I fight
To reach the light.
If the darkness
Takes me prisoner
I will never
See light again.

Sleep

Slipping into sleep
With my family close by to comfort me,
I thank the world for its rich treasures
And I celebrate the time I had awake
And I feel the light fade out of me,
Releasing me from pain.

Slipping peacefully into sleep
I ache for the night that is to come;
I fear nothing that lies in front of me,
Nor regret a moment that I've lived through
Nor will I try to keep at bay the sleep
That takes me far from here.

Swift and peaceful comes this sleep
As I am encircled by the familiar sounds
That gave me pleasure in those fantastic days;
The laughter, the questions, the easy answers.
The answer for me is now clear and plain –
I will slip away as sleep slips quietly in.

John J Whitmarsh

John did have his wish, and slipped quietly away during his sleep on 4th April 2004.

Paula Brown

John J. Whitmarsh by Karin Sköld

More work by John J Whitmarsh may be found at:

http://temptme-at.4t.com
http://www.thepeoplespoet.com

other works by John J Whitmarsh

Magic Light 0-9543621-2-8 £7.50 + £2.50 P&P from the Publisher, Paula Brown

paulabrownpublishing@btinternet.com

Paula Brown
1a Bright Road

Paula Brown Publishing
26 Uplands Road, Drayton
Portsmouth, Hampshire
PO6 1HS U.K.

John has also written a number of novels, yet to be published.

Message

Listen this one last time
To the words of a man
Who is determined to display
The sum of his meaning
On the canvas of your ear –
I
Loved
You.

John J Whitmarsh